MW01234798

Silence, Inhabited

Poetic Reflections on
Surviving Childhood Sexual Abuse

Rich Follett

NeoPoiesis Press, LLC

NeoPoiesis Press
P.O. Box 38037
Houston, Texas 77238-8037
www.neopoiesispress.com

Silence, Inhabited: Poetic Reflections on
Surviving Childhood Sexual Abuse
by Rich Follett
ISBN 978-0-9819984-9-7 (paperback : alk. paper)
        1. Poetry. I. Follett, Rich

Printed in the United States of America

First Edition

Also by Rich Follett and Constance Stadler

Responsorials
Copyright 2009, published by NeoPoiesis Press, LLC
ISBN 978-0-9819984-3-5

This body of work would never have existed if not for the
patience, faith and courage of my beloved wife
Mary Ruth Alred Follett.

Her steadfast determination to outlast and overcome the myriad
dæmons and ghosts borne of my survival has made the difference
for me between living fully and merely existing.

My lengthening periods of wellness – of wholeness –
may be traced directly to her fortitude and dedication.

It is because of Mary Ruth that I found the strength to find
my voice at last.

Even on the darkest days (there are many, still) I never forget
how truly blessed I am to love and to be loved
by such an extraordinary human being.

Contents

Foreword

In February of 2009, my life was about to change.

I did not know it at the time, for what was commencing had the external earmarks of a familiar routine spanning more than a score of years – it was the first session of a new poetry workshop. As the participants cautiously filed in, I immediately saw someone I recognized; a rarity in that I was a newcomer to this small hamlet in Northern Virginia.

Rich Follett is a much-loved citizen of 'The Shenandoah'; with a crystalline tenor voice; he is also its resident minstrel and a respected local actor. I was delighted to have a real artist in the mix. Then the hammer fell: he graciously explained that he and his wife Mary Ruth had made a mistake - they thought they were attending a poetry *reading*.

The preliminary gestures of retreat were being made, but there was no question: he must *not* leave. It mattered. After a bit of pedagogical 'maneuvering', the Folletts stayed.

During that first 'getting to know all' discussion, Rich revealed that he had not written a word of poetry for thirty years. He then relayed the all too familiar (but never sadder) story of a revered professor slashing his judgmental axe and proclaiming a burgeoning young writer terminally 'bad'. I sensed the anguish of a deeply sensitive, spiritual soul – this decades-old declaration struck me as an incompetent condemnation demanding intervention.

After covering some of the fundamentals, I gave an assignment: "Choose a poem you love and write a response." Rich chose Pulitzer prize-winning Virginia native Henry Taylor's *Barbed Wire*, a beautiful poem about observing the slow, agonizing death of an impaled stallion. Rich returned with his response: *Barbed Mirror* – an account of the same incident as experienced by the majestic, doomed animal.

It took all the composure I had to not gasp in the presence of the other attendees. In my hands were the words of a poetic genius. These are the closing stanzas:

with each of my merest movements,
(masterpieces of sublime fluidity), i
flustered the old men into dim longing,
their shame-bound, tobacco-stained hisses
echoing the remembered hitch in their loins
on summer nights a haggard generation removed from
the stagnant swelter of this, my dying day
it was an unexpected whinny on the wind, perhaps: a neigh; a nicker;
far off, a filly or foal gamboling in the wanton apricot aura of afternoon;
or, possibly, the careless clash of man and machine; some aimless, nameless noise -

i was grazing, gazing at the men with leaf-brown faces
when some glimmer of
gut-wrenching ingrained genetic detritus
spurred me to wild, consanguine flight

my winged hooves against my will,
i was racing, raking along rows of stannic briars;
garroted as green grass ran red -
as the old men's leathery laughter lashed me on to oblivion

with the hemic buzz of my silvered slaughter
hung in the air like rustling sheaves,
i lowered my head to reproach their gaping faces;
the shriveling, tractor-plowed masks of those drying, dying men –
they who in a lifetime of barren labor had known but a moment's grace
in the frenzied grip of perfidious procreation

it was then
in that mirrored moment
when at last

 i flew...

We moved into the depths of exploration, trenches of emotion and revelation of the carnage. I began to see a pattern in Rich's writing – writing so perfect that I almost never made a single correction. A deeply bruised heart, clenched for decades, was opening up in aching increments. With each new write, another facet of this gorgeous, wrenching portrait was added. I remember well the amazing genesis of *sensitivity suite*:

We were doing sensory isolations. Each student was blindfolded and asked to dip his hand into one of three plastic bags containing three substances. Smell was not permitted; touch was all. Rich had not attended the class that evening, so Mary Ruth took a copy of the 'ingredients list' home and did the exercise with him later. Here I paraphrase her words, related to me in a tremulous, astonished voice: 'He put his hand into the first bag and almost immediately withdrew it; the exact same process was repeated when he inserted his hand into the remaining two. He then ran up the stairs and began writing for hours.' What resulted shook Rich so much that he needed to have Mary Ruth at his side in order to be able to share it.

In each of the three parts of the finished work, I saw the relation to the catalyst, but the depths of soul exposure and the ineffable beauty of the composition made the listener feel as if splayed in the presence of some divinity. Rich tells the story of his life as a brutally abused, damaged soul in the making: in the first part, the wantonly cruel, blatantly self-serving deceits of a fiercely manipulative and narcissistic father are revealed; in the second, struggles to begin a fledging acting career in the face of hardship and in the wake of years of abuse are recounted in all their penetrative horror; in the third, a funeral parlor viewing of his dead brother - a suicide by shotgun - concludes the triptych with a horrifying absolute that echoes the nightmare of his upbringing:

i had to look at what was there
at what was left
the freckles across the nose were darker
there were more of them than i remembered
the eye was no longer the color of the sea
but it did slant upwards at the corner like a grin
yes, i concluded
this was him
i was just about to look away
when something moved –
breathlessly i waited, praying
for his last trick to be real
for him to sit up
for his ocean eyes to twinkle

it was a maggot

i am okay with that

Once the gates were open, Rich's courageous spirit poured forth and one of the finest writers I have had the privilege to read took full form. No aspect of the ramifications of being reared as a victim of the vilest crimes that can be inflicted on a child was omitted. *keep* told the tale of the pain that lies beneath the stones of humiliated secrecy, of the unscreamed torture behind the imprisonment of an eviscerated, supremely violated childhood:

in these stones
dwell memories i never countenanced
experiences unbidden
rushing the brim of despair

they are not vacant

in these stones
stay secrets i sequester
bound by mortar, the work of man
prisoners of wild, witless will

they are not inert

in these stones
seethe unseeming desires i smother

they are not of God

In bloodied, soft tones, *weight* detailed torturous memories
and took us inside the mind of a child desperately trying to
cope with and understand his serial brutalization:

as a wide-eyed nine-year old
in the canned goods aisle of the local IGA

a musky presence fumbled from behind
as i was carried
through flapping, filmy, filthy thermal fringe
to a back alley

minutes-like-hours later,
a grimy quarter was pressed into my hand
with a slumbering admonition –
be a good boy and don't tell.

As Rich grew in strength and voice, the exhumation went
deeper. In *Pimp of the Perverse,* the story of an actor whose
'freak' alter-ego is being paraded on stage as a spectacle, *every*
maddening inner voice is released. To read such monumental
tragedy and not feel blistered raw by the experience goes
beyond the circumference of 'being human'. The twisted
anomaly of the near-destroyed is confronted by another inner
voice in the character of his 'manager' – the self-condemner
and sadistic instrument of the most barbaric interior
Inquisition imaginable:

For years now
you've been telling anyone who'll listen
how you've devoted your life to healing and forgiveness

(thank God for expert therapy and good drugs);

you've fooled the masses;
dazzled the critics;
bowing nightly to your own tumescent hype –

you dickless, simpering poseur

To call this a book of magnificent poetry would be wildly inadequate. While it *is* that, it is also much more. On this journey, we travel with the poet on a most complex, *believable* path from a childhood filled with the vilest horrors to an adulthood steeped in healing grace. It is a wonder to behold; it is a wonder as well to arrive so firmly in the knowledge that this work will help thousands who have endured such abuse and who seek affirmation to begin walking or the strength to *continue* walking on similar paths.

I have reviewed hundreds of books of poetry; *Silence, Inhabited* is a once-in-a-lifetime work of heart and of art. This is the quintessential symbiosis of beauty and unspeakable horror. While it is not an easy read, it is an *essential* read, and it is requisite for the reader to remember what the writer endured in order to be able to create such a transformational volume of work. There can no question that the reader will be changed by this book, humbled by its infinitely beautiful power and deeply stirred by its immense humanity.

Constance Stadler Ph.D., editor, author, *Tinted Steam, Sublunary Curse, Paper Cuts, Rummaging in the Attic,* and *Responsorials* (with Rich Follett)

Introduction

"Out of suffering have emerged the strongest souls; the most massive characters are seared with scars."
Kahlil Gibran

I began to write this collection of poems long before the first word appeared on paper. I began to write *Silence, Inhabited* on the day (a date lost to history, obscured by a haze of pain and self-destructive behaviors) when I first pondered the possibility that the legacy of horror which begat my overwhelming desire to be *heard* might, in its cataclysmic wake, bear the seeds of untold benisons – that the crippling rage borne of my stolen innocence and lost boyhood might herald an auspicious opportunity to discover real strengths, insights and intuitions which never would have existed but for the need to *survive*.

My story has all of the malignant markers one would expect to find in the malevolent lexicon of childhood sexual abuse; as an adolescent, I ached to share the myriad mournful, secret particulars with a trusted guide who would either exorcise my demons or rescue me from them. It has taken every day of the years since (and the expert help of *many* trusted guides) for me to fully comprehend that only *I* am capable of demon-slaying within the sphere of my remembered personal experience. Have I gained sufficient strength and confidence to divulge the litany of my woundings – to expose the scars that Gibran would have us believe are indicative of a 'massive character'? Certainly. In practice, however, such a spectacle would be antithetical to any real understanding of what is intended to speak from these pages. It has been both the greatest revelation and the greatest irony of my journey that the dire story I wanted so desperately for people to *hear* throughout my boyhood and adolescence has been rendered moot by the emboldened vista the man I have become endeavors to engender.

There *are* a few mileposts, essential to a reader's comprehension of the overarching schema, which I will list here:

- I was sexually abused outside of my home repeatedly by a male caregiver (and, later, by others) from infancy until shortly after my fifteenth birthday
- As a child, I attempted to share these incidents with trusted adults who either could not conceive of or refused to believe in their actuality
- As an adolescent/young adult, I placed myself frequently and purposefully in situations which invited repetition (or, at the least, imitation) of the abuses I had endured in childhood, thereby perpetuating and strengthening their influence upon my emerging identity
- I possessed only shadowy recall of the majority of the early childhood incidents until my primary abuser died, at which point the memories became crystalline and newly terrifying
- Although I am now free of many of the self-destructive behaviors which undermined my early efforts to find peace within myself and in the world, I am still struggling daily to remain steadfast and balanced
- I have been working toward forgiveness - for myself and for my abusers – for more than thirty years and acknowledge unequivocally that the greater part of the journey will *always* lie before me

Within the lines and images of *Silence, Inhabited* dwell a toddler's blown innocence, a lost boy's anguished cry for help, a suicidal adolescent's rage at having failed three times to end the life of the monster within, a young man's evanescent entreaty for good to spring from the ashes of evil, a grown man's crippling shame and the blessed relief of a senescent sophist's ineluctable acceptance. According to Shakespeare, I still have an age and a half to go. Thank you for sharing my journey – each of you brings hope and affirmation.

~ Rich Follett, January 2010

keep

in these stones
live truths i never told

they are not dead

in these stones
abide surreptitious, crepuscular echoes
of my stifled, stolen innocence
lost before it could be reckoned
stillborn on the cusp of perfection

they are not mute

in these stones
lie tears i never cried
glimmering harbingers of feckless hope;
fountains staunched by the eidolon survival -

they are not barren

in these stones
in *each* of these stones
rests a shard of glorious promise
shattered by the quietus
of my numberless, perdurable aborted screams

they are not insensible

in these stones
lurk shades i leave unanswered
importuning corporeal justice
from passersby

they are not cold

in these stones
dwell memories i never countenanced
experiences unbidden
rushing the brim of despair

they are not vacant

in these stones
stay secrets i sequester
bound by mortar, the work of man
prisoners of wild, witless will

they are not inert

in these stones
seethe unseeming desires i smother

they are not of God

self, savaged, seven

i will not die before my death

i will not settle for

      putrefaction and spiritual half life

i will not drink

      the malevolent venom of petty revenge

when i arch my back

(and i *will* arch my back,

as it pleases you...)

the beckoning curve will bespeak

      promise

          pleasure

             passion

all for you

my defiler

i will become most fully alive

only in your saurian clutch

i will live,

in this moment of your squalid satisfaction,

more life than you will ever know

in the full diapason

       of your fetid conquests

i am now

ever was

ever shall be

woven of the fabric of forgiveness

my warp and weft

substantiated with each infertile thrust

you are waning

as i rise

i fly

as you flagellate

       your flaccid fantasies...

grunt;

  sweat;

    swear;

you will have no sway

in pursuit of

the precious, perceived innocence

i lost long ago

i am empty

blown before the first bud

you cannot fill me

with your rage

today

i am your atrophied angel;

tomorrow

when you tire of me

i will write poems

newly chaste in their truth –

each word

a belated epitaph

to

fear

sensitivity suite

i.

i am eight
on a sand bar
which
like me
only appears – only comes out –
when the tide is low and all is calm

my father has left me alone
'wait here and swim' he said;
dropped me down
and sped off
(who imagined the old boat's propeller could turn so fast?)....
apparently
there is a girl in a white bikini
near the mouth of the inlet
screaming out to the open sea
dad to the rescue
'son, wait here...'
dad to the rescue
my sand bar is sinking

she, grateful, hugs him
he lingers in her embrace a long moment past awkward
before ceding her to the singing beach
all the way back to the dock he will tell me
how her name was merrie lee
how unusual that was
how impressed he was with her character
character my eight-year-old ass
you son of a bitch

like that sand bar
the whole business was beneath me
but i clung to shrinking, shifting sands
just to keep breathing

near the end i went under
water more than two feet deep now
and beginning to move fast
i lay on the bottom
(the bottom that only moments ago had been the top)
i let out all of my air and
lay motionless – looking toward heaven –
breathing in a new element
thinking those fluke were really onto something
breathing happily in a new element
until i found myself inexplicably aloft and sputtering...

that he came back for me at all
continues to surprise

we had been fishing, father and i
outboard set to troll
i hovered over the rotting transom to steer and to spy
feeling the motor's heat
envying joan of arc
so clean an ending – so incontrovertible
(they say her heart did not burn)

my true purpose in this faux-halcyon escapade
was to look
through the clearer-than-you'd-think-it-would-be water
clear down to the bottom
to spot marbles
marbles you see
are the eyes of a mythical fluke buried in the sand
bigger than a volkswagen, says dad
old flat poseidon
he is down there somewhere
and my father ahab
will see him rendered in strips
battered (how appropriate words can be without knowing)
and served up with ore-ida's finest
at our family's rendition of the perfect friday dinner
'round the table

amen
norman rockwell would have been proud
but scratch the canvas and you'll find we were bosch
painted over
in suburban teal and burnt orange

so i called out 'marbles!' as we trolled
and dad would drop the hook right down
up came fish after fish
hooray
sportsmanship for assholes

every fish was smaller than expected
every summer friday a bit closer to the fall
disappointment was my father's condiment of choice

i learned in the sixth grade
that fluke, like their smaller cousin the flounder
(*flounder*? how could we not have known?)
begin life with two eyes on opposite sides of their head
like any other fish
then, slowly,
in an effort to avoid being seen and eaten
they flatten
and both eyes migrate to the side of their body that looks
toward heaven

smart fish

i helped them, you know
i called out only the barest few, and then only
to avoid being seen
to avoid being captured
to avoid being rendered in strips
to avoid being battered and served up
to postpone the burgeoning, insatiable chagrin

even today
when the tide rushes in

i bury myself in the sand
and look toward heaven
waiting for my eyes to migrate

ii.

these pebbles –
lava from a volcano
that exploded a whole lot of thousands of years ago
nowhere near arizona
where i am now
after riding a bus for three days
to an acting job my parents said i shouldn't take

fuck them

i am seventeen
i hop a big apple greyhound on christmas eve
the peter pan touring company is the key to my nascent career
in lights
but on the way
mister dumbass producer skips town with the money
one blinding incomprehensible greedy twist of balding sweaty
mama's-boy fate
and my incandescent debut turns out to be
just another case of 'my parents were right'

i wait in the phoenix bus station
it is three in the morning
no one has come to claim me

my doppelganger walks up,
says 'are you here for the peter pan touring company?'
'it's about fucking time', i say;
only to hear 'no – i am stuck here, too' and
suddenly it all becomes clear –
he is bob

from somewhere vast and flat

we are soon joined by a third
named larry
he is heir to the kodak fortune
(no, really – i checked later)
he is a peter pan touring company rising star
like bob,
like me…
his parents turned out to be right, as well –
(bob doesn't have parents
but if he did, they'd be ri…)

fuck them
fuck them all

we do not have enough money for bus tickets home
we consider selling ourselves
we'd have done it, too
but that only would have made our parents more right

fuck them
fuck them all

greyhound ad says 'buy two, get one free'
holiday special
we pool our resources
who knows who, where?
i win; my cousin's in l.a.

we three
salvaged by cousin tom in a dented orange pinto
lived in his garage
for six months
sleeping on and under a ping-pong table
and eating avocados fresh from a tree in the backyard
eden without eve –
one night
we fumbled clumsily with each other in her absence,

deciding in the end we were better off sans satisfaction

two weeks into the eden experiment
proving once and for all that i am my pragmatic parents' son
i borrow a bicycle
i ride each day to the redondo beach boardwalk
where i sell flowers in an open air market
i get this job
solely because albert the owner's son desires me –
sycophantic albert, whose middle name was futility...
i sold only flowers
(once, to olivia newton-john,
a single red rose
she was so...pretty)

bob went back to his vast flatness;
larry, to claim his diseased fortune –
i held out 'til the last
feasting on pride

fuck them
fuck them all

my mother's quavering mouse-voice on the telephone
she is worried about me
have i been drinking?

so i cave
i fly back to new york
(much quicker than greyhound)
i would say i missed home but
you read my last poem
three weeks later my cousin called to say he had not seen me –
had i come home

three weeks?

fuck him
fuck them all

14

thirty years later
a quiet moment draws me back to
these pebbles –
lava from a volcano
that exploded a whole lot of thousands of years ago
nowhere near arizona
where i am now
if only in my mind

if only

i

had been able to explode...

iii.

i insisted on seeing my brother's body
it nearly killed my parents
it nearly killed me
but see it i did
(the one thing we had in common,
my brother and i –
we were born to ruin)

he was lying on his right side
one eye gazing opaquely outward
the other half of his face
covered by a starched white cloth
i asked to see
the other half of his face
to make sure it was there
to make sure it was him

he was always a trickster
i asked to see the other half
of his dappled face
and they told me it wasn't there to see

the shotgun had done its work
(who knew his arms were so long?)

i had to look at what was there
at what was left
the freckles across the nose were darker
there were more of them than i remembered
the eye was no longer the color of the sea
but it did slant upwards at the corner like a grin
yes, i concluded
this was him

i was just about to look away
when something moved –

breathlessly i waited, praying
for his last trick to be real
for him to sit up
for his ocean eyes to twinkle

it was a maggot

i am okay with that

weight

i.

most of all
i remember being held down;

riding my bike
and then

on top of me
(never *above* me – not for a moment)
suffocating, excruciating weight

ghoulish, contorted masks -

many in succession;
(many more, once the word got out...)

i knew them, i am sure
knew each of them
sometimes i knew their names
sometimes their faces
but i did not know
not then
not now
(never knew - not for a moment)
their reasons
for feeding on pain
pain for themselves
pain for others

as a wide-eyed nine-year old
in the canned goods aisle of the local IGA

a musky presence fumbled from behind
as i was carried
through flapping, filmy, filthy thermal fringe
to a back alley

18

minutes-like-hours later,
a grimy quarter was pressed into my hand
with a slumbering admonition –
be a good boy and don't tell.

i did not tell;
could not have told –

i only told my mother i had found a quarter

'a <u>whole</u> quarter?'

'i'm not sure, mother...

it has no face.'

ii.

many missing faces and
two decades later

i learned to disappear

although i could no longer feel the weight,

in quiet moments

i pondered whether or not
Bernoulli's principle
applied to the human form

dreaming all the while
of tall buildings
and release

i did not understand
(never understood - not for a moment)

how i could invite the faceless ones
when others like them had caused so much pain

how i could keep inviting them
again and again

here
now
so long after
the weight had gone

as a child
i could not resist;

no longer a child,
i could not desist -

disappearing had become so easy

i did not see
(never saw - not for a moment)
that i had a choice...

they followed me,
the faceless ones, and

i followed them –
i disappeared nightly;

they never did

iii.

once

in the twilight
between decades

(just once)

i took a deep breath
and, hovering in the limbo between
helplessness and invisibility,

watched myself say

no

watched as

the monosyllabic archangel of my nascent redemption
escaped my blown lips
only to be snuffed out
by the weight of a grimy hand

try as i might

i could no longer disappear

i stayed, then
raping myself anew in my silence

i did not cry
(never cried – not for a moment)

Bernoulli was a charlatan

iv.

one stifled summer sunday
i flipped that faceless quarter;
that badge of crippling cowardice,
now a talisman of misbegotten Providence –

flipped once
(tails!)

and began a crime spree

shoplifting only what i did not need;
sneaking it all back later

distracting turgid, thick-waisted security guards
with anonymous. androgynous whispered solicitations

in my fantasies
they ran me down

they punished me

i did not consider
(never considered – not for a moment)
the possibility of a life without fear

this ended
as unexpectedly as it had begun

on the winged, leaden morning
when first i considered the possibility
of an identity
without fear

v.

now
middle-aged
stout
happily married

i am
a teacher –
respected, revered

living abundant dreams (nightmares' progeny)

having long since forgiven my silent former self –

as it turns out

i did not believe
not then
not now
(never believed – not for a moment)
that the faceless ones
were inside me to stay

now that they no longer appear

now that i no longer disappear

now that i

my own archangel

have ascended...

i,

reborn,

ponder Bernoulli

and struggle

with

weight

Pimp of the Perverse

pssssssssssssst ...

You.

Victim.

Boy Wonder.

Pedophile's puppet.

You hear me,
I know you do.

You *liked* it, didn't you?

Delectable, ineluctable;
a *petit mal* serial melodrama of repugnant submission –
that final furtive flush of excruciating, exquisite surrender
calls to you still.

That's your big secret, isn't it, freak?

For years now
you've been telling anyone who'll listen
how you've devoted your life to healing and forgiveness
(thank God for expert therapy and good drugs);

you've fooled the masses;
dazzled the critics;
bowing nightly to your own tumescent hype –

you dickless, simpering poseur

(oh, save the feigned indignation –
we knew all along).

Still;

what a fucking production!

Tonight,
on the occasion of your umpteenth triumphant performance,
your supporting cast has gathered
to honor you with an après matinée toast.

You may recall Hoover,
the chorus girl?
She can suck the chrome off a hubcap
without smearing her lipstick.
How many times has she finished a scene
when you choked?

And this is UPS Guy –
the stage manager –
whenever you needed to look great in shorts
or accept deliveries at the rear
he never missed his cue.

Butch
(your straight man)
is here, too:
always happy to take the fall
when stock gags failed to entertain and
the garish light of truth threatened to expose your artless
farce.

Lorelei,
(your understudy)
still waits in the wings
if ever you feel unsafe, unsure.
If ever it seemed you couldn't go on,
she always found you a new leading man – *different* –
with strong, sheltering arms
to keep you from being afraid in the presence of all the others
(it was just a touch of stage fright now and again).
She'd rehearse him into a lather
and turn him right over to you

for the climax
(before he sensed how the plot had twisted).
Lorelei,
now appearing:
one night only –
it has really always been *her* show.

They're all here for you, kid ...
you've been with each of them;
you've *been* each of them.
Oh ... me?
I'm your agent,
remember?
The Pimp of the Perverse.
I pull the strings;
I run the whole goddamn show.

See this contract?
I *own* you.

Pathetic parasite –
you were nobody when I found you;
you'd be nobody still, if ...

Well, never mind.
this is an open-ended engagement,
the box office is boffo
and your adoring public waits.

Just don't get any big ideas about retirement

(let us merely say
I'd be willing, if necessary, to tell the press
your tastes once ran to the...exotic).

Goodness, how 'bout that time?
They're seating for the evening show already!

On stage, Olivier.

27

Try not to trip over the scenery.

Ladies and Gentlemen,

GIMCRACK THEATRE

is proud to present ...

exculpation

boy,
i *see* you:
once, i *was* you.

i cannot heal you.

(even if i could,
you are years away
from finding truth
in my admonitions).

any connection i might make
would reveal in me the same lascivious light
that emanated from the tortured eyes
of he who first set me to howling –

any consolation i might afford
would diminish your capacity
to recognize future defilers,
impugning my higher purpose.

i can offer only this,
my indirect benediction ...

you will soon begin a journey
(in truth, you have already begun).

you will never know your destination.

the map is a lie.

everyone you meet will speak in riddles.

those unlike you will not understand you,
nor will you understand them;
those like you will feast upon your affliction.

29

rescuers with God in their eyes
will not prove equal
to the task of your redemption,
for they will not see
the mark of shame upon you;
well-meaning prophets of Baal
offer no comfort beyond *now* –
the time you lose in their embrace
can never be regained.

you will *always* blame yourself ...

your despoiler?

fear him not;
he has forgotten you –
he is plowing fresher fields
(you have already yielded innocence,
which cannot be sown on the same ground twice).

scavengers, whose heinous debauchery will follow
(sometimes at your request),
though their taloned scythes be just as sharp –
are merely demons
looming to vanish the instant you call them
by their rightful name.

gradually,
you will purge your predilection
for the familiarity of their abominations.

within you, a tarnished moral compass
flickers toward true North and hope;
though its magnetism will never again be immaculate,
still it will reckon, once you learn its terms ...

above all, your brokenness
must remain uncompromised;
its potency is the only insurance

against execrable perpetuation
of the horrors that have shaped you.

in due course, you will come to understand
that nothing can be what you would wish
but some things –
some precious few –
may be what you will *need*
if only you learn to recognize
the impress of truth upon them.

it is time.

your restlessness
heralds incipient manhood.

go now,
but know:

this will never be finished.

any faith you invest
in believing the curse can be reversed –
in believing the past can be forgotten –
is folly.

your only achievable victory lies
in steadfast, righteous vigilance.

you must transmogrify
your lust for vengeance;
let grief engender a gyre of grace
lest humanity forsake you
ere you receive Eleos' gifts
borne on the wings
of survival.

as a violin sings
only when bowed by its tormentor,

so must you scream honor
in the clutch of remembered evil ...

long after ghost fingers have ceased
their corrupt carnal caress,
one true chord will linger –
as its echoed anthem emerges,
your anguished ears will attune to the cry
of a waiting warrior.

become *that* man.

become a man
who could never do
what lesser men did
to the boy you were.

become a man
who knows
that boy you were
can never be healed.

become a man
who knows
that boy
can only be

forgiven.

in defense of the violin

poor tormented rebec;
instrument of acoustic crucifixion –
agonistes under horsehair lash,
writhing;
vainly imploring olympus for absolution.

in chaotic fusillade,
goaded by the maestro's masseteric baton,
pimpled protégé saws,
drawing prow of bow
across sinews stretched to insanity.

racked and pegged for maximum torque,
fretting and fettered,
cacophony borne of colophony;
stricken strings singing out defiance:
symphonic hieronymous bosch.

amati; stradivari; guarneri;
suffixes, merely:
was not the pochette sufficient?

thus, violin begat viol:
promethean strains
rising; falling; dying;
necrotic nectar
slathered in fetid excess
upon gobbets of culture's corpse,
consumed by caterwauling critics
(later, vomited
to be re-devoured by lesser hearers).

many generations since
have waxed rhapsodic
in the rapture of vibrating gut;
i, for one, echo the bard:

my soul shall ne'er be haled from my body
by bridged bellwether bowel.

strange, brother benedick?

is it not, rather,
utterly befitting
that a civilization forged in folly
and basest inhumanity
should find sublimest satisfaction –
most beatific beauty –
in the sound of feral feline entrails
splayed across martyred heartwood,
abraded to aural anguish
by the proud plume of a horse's ass?

in every birth, perhaps,
a presage of death;
in every pleasured moan
the augural knell of impending eternity ...

we live to die;
we die to live;

all the while, hovering
in the barely perceptible balance
(a prophetic mosquito in irony's ear),
nero's darling
intones the inevitable ...

silence, inhabited

obmutescence

      begins with a murmured, malevolent charge:

be a good boy –
              don't tell ...

an amaclæan nursery rhyme –

           mephitic, mesmerizing ...

eroded, grimy quarter pressed into wide-eyed palm;

              the chafed nether-ooze of felched probity;

                  outwardly imperceptible,

                        visceral plate tectonics churn

engendering castrating, basal revulsion –

              an inchoate mantle of unworthiness formed

              as boyhood's prepuce is extirpated.

numberless, voiceless deceptions will follow.

in time, perineal outrage will subside;

the numbing of a soul

takes longer.

ii.

in the aftermath of *magnum malum,*

       ectoplasmic blown innocence

            (sulfurous, ulcerous haze)

     gluts fetid air –

a halo of incontinent brimstone

               stinking of spiritual death.

at the omphalos,

      an aphonic wraith

        adrift in incredulity

          clutching referent shards –

antæus had earth;

     i, silence.

iii.

in the pedophile's wake,

psychic armageddon:

rage is insufficient;

hatred, absurdly comic –

any appropriate response

vaporizes in virulent waves of self-mockery.

a child's physiognomy,

ill-suited to shaping tragedy's mask,

defaults to manic laughter

and the desperate pursuit of approbation –

the only panacea for sullying shame.

in the absence of jettisoned self,

(buoyancy is survival)

being a *good boy* becomes all:

being a *good boy*

for father, brother, friend, lover,

(the lines blur)

sister, mother, god and others –

being a *good boy*

means warmth and shelter.

being a *good boy*

means safety.

for fleeting moments,

catalogued, cloistered and cosseted,

being a *good boy*

anaesthetizes the demons within ...

iv.

in a parallel universe

my faustian doppelganger

wagers his soul

not to know,

but to *forget.*

of this, i am sure.

it's a losing game

either way:

diabolus

will have his due;

the outcome

is inevitable.

why, then

do we persist –

straining to decipher

the book of spells

40

in a tempest

when every flash of

lightning

leaves us

newly blind?

the fabric

of a boyhood

rent by rape

can never again

auger

warp from weft –

will never again

weave true.

this certainty

that nothing can be

as it was

arrives spasmodically,

in phantasmic bolts

of strobe-lit mania.

hope's chimeric,

errant strands

beckon

even as the abyss

swallows

aborted promise.

between

lightning reveals,

faust bargains;

diabolus dances ...

v.

unassaugeable,

relentless,

indefatigable,

slavering, baying;

culpability

pursues –

a pack of curséd curs

snarling, snapping,

scenting conquest

of soul - of sanity.

what purpose, then, in flight?

do we not attract

the inexorable destiny

best befitting our

basest aberrations?

nevertheless;

nearer to god,

on a rocky crag,

clinging to the gnarled,

upturned scions

of a stunted,

self-loathing tree

(guilt candelabra),

a battered boy waits –

praying for rescue

by the hero

he might one day become.

against reason,

against hope,

even as cerberus circles,

a terrified tremolo ascends,

beseeching deliverance;

imploring the inconceivable:

mens sibi conscia recti.

vi.

in the absence of light,

darkness becomes familiar;

in the comfort of the void,

complacency masquerades as redemption.

virtue, untimely stripped

in plundered stygian intercourse,

craves absolution –

waste no time

waiting

for a still, small voice

(stifled spleen

does not signify serenity).

act.

reach.

truth is aerobic;

light

follows the will

to live.

vii.

it is only in making peace

    with the permanence of loss

        that healing happens;

only in accepting

    the immutability of helplessness

        that revivification begins.

innocence, stolen, wields a new death

in every intimate moment:

outrage (molestation's miscreant offspring) wails,

freshly wounded, with each tendered tomorrow ...

to annul the violator's legacy,

    embrace the victim within:

to vilify is to venerate –

45

to revile the defiler; to vitiate anew.

forgiveness reflects and refracts,

    radiating outward from

        the metamorphosed vortex of guilt

    (transform the core to abjure the corruption).

if you wish to live, let loathing die –

    this is the call of lost boys waiting

to be summoned from the depths of soundless shame –

    to shatter secrecy with a righteous manhood

        plucked from the maw of despair.

silence, inhabited:

stigma's valediction;

resurrection's surest song ...

meum alium corpus

i.

terra

to be, but for a moment,

    a sparrow above the maelstrom;

    one resplendent featherlight ray of faltering promise

to refute Armageddon;

to witness creation and destruction dancing;

to catch, aloft

    the aching fulgent fortissimo

        of this teeming, besotted rondure;

to savor the merest morsel of Gaia's grand score –

this would suffice!

refrain;

strain;

musical terms both –

by whose flawed design did they come to apply

to something so quintessentially *free*?

earthbound, i feign animus

drawing sluggish sausages across insouciant strings

perchance to seduce the sparrow?

'...*that strain again;*

it had a dying fall...'

strain, indeed –

         let it die,

            let it fall,

but *do* refrain.

no Segovia, i.

              ii.

             aer

a fritillary

floating beyond the reach of

earth's ponderous pavane

flitting effortlessly above the gyre;

       no need of voice

when every flutter is Art!

exponentially ignorant,

i, wailing Icarus,

disseminate a tremulous tenor

in the papillon's wake

a meager, miscreant mimic

keening senselessly,

keenly oblivious to my own arrogance-

'...*a wandering minstrel, i...*'

wander, then.

iii.

ignis

a hurdy gurdy, it seems

or perhaps call–and-response calliopes

would sooner flank sweet Heaven

than my fawning, masturbatory lays-

how, then, to vault

the confine

of my menial muse?

verily, i burn

for want of one requited utterance!

an echo without origination

languishing in lieu of purpose

i bounce infinitely

      reaffirming my own creative redundancy

         with each reverberation

in desperation now, i dance –

(that which has no voice cannot offend God's ear)

 whirling

     swirling

      twirling

i am Baryshnikov, at the very least -

'dance, dance, wherever you may be...'

until the thundering pulse of my leaden footfalls

betrays my winged spirit –

gravity is in effect today.

iv.

undae

if i left this minute;

circumnavigated the globe -

i could watch my tears go down the drain

clockwise in one hemisphere

counterclockwise in the other

who cares which way or where

it would just be so damned dramatic

Coriolis performance art!

'*if you look closer, it's easy to trace*

the tracks of m-'

just to be sure

i google my tears

virtually test my hypothesis

only to learn

they diffuse

according to their own peevish whims

regardless

of longitude.

well, *shit.*

v.

spiritus

dentist's office;

new-age acoustic anesthesia

wafts with Bose brilliance

bringing blessed numbness

beneath it all

inexplicable one-ness

imperceptible, nearly,

but...there... *there.*

i shuffle back through æons of genetic memory

through the ominous groaning of an impending root canal

past the pain

past the pathos

past caring

burying all consciousness in pursuit of the divine mystery

beneath the pan-pipes

beneath the waves

beneath the elemental thrum -

whale song.

my song, too.

earth; air; fire; water –

        one.

i know, now.

i strum

    i sing

      i dance

        i cry

all at once -

and in this

        (only in this)

my life-poem

        i am a child again.

in this

        my one true song

borne on spirit wings;

        trembling -

            i touch

                the sun…

Rich Follett has recently returned to writing poetry after a thirty-year hiatus. He lives in the sacred and timeless Shenandoah Valley of Virginia, where he joyfully teaches English and Theatre Arts for high school students. His poems have appeared in numerous contemporary journals and e-zines including *BlazeVox, Paraphilia, Exercise Bowler, Calliope Nerve, Sugar Mule, Four Branches Press and Counterexample Poetics*, for which he is a Featured Artist. He is the co-author of *Responsorials* (with Constance Stadler). Most recently, his haiku/photo combination *Aurora's Adieu* received first place honors in the first international iPoetry Poe-Tography Competition.

Permissions & Acknowledgements

These poems have previously been published by Calliope Nerve, Counterexample Poetics, Four Branches Press, and Paraphilia.

Photo Credits:

Page xi: Doug Sanford
Page 24: Ron Godby
Page 28: Bonnie Sprung
Page 36: Robin Flanagan O'Driscoll
Prior Page: John Westervelt

All other photographs are presented herein on behalf of the Author.

Reflections

NeoPoiesis
a new way of making

in ancient Greece, poiesis referred to the process of making
creation – production – organization – formation – causation
a process that can be physical and spiritual
biological and intellectual
artistic and technological
material and teleological
efficient and formal
a means of modifying the environment
and a method of organizing the self
the making of art and music and poetry
the fashioning of memory and history and philosophy
the construction of perception and expression and reality

NeoPoiesis Press
reflecting the creative drive and spirit
of the new electronic media environment

LaVergne, TN USA
01 February 2011
214825LV00001B/160/P